# There's a Hole in the Bucket

# There's a Hole in the Bucket

pictures by Nadine Bernard Westcott

HarperCollins*Publishers*

Westcott, Nadine Bernard.
     There's a hole in the bucket / by Nadine Bernard Westcott.
        p.        cm.
     Summary: As Liza instructs Henry how to fix a
hole in the bucket, Henry gives her all the reasons
why he can't. An illustrated version of a humorous
old folk song.
     ISBN 0-06-026422-5
     ISBN 0-06-026423-3 (lib. bdg.)
     1. Folk songs—Texts.   [1. Folk songs.
     2. Pails—Folklore.]   I. Title.
     PZ8.3.W4998Th 1990    89-34538
     782.42162'0026'8—dc20   CIP
                        AC

Lyrics copyright © 1974 by Marie Winn and Allen Miller
from *The Fireside Book of Fun & Game Songs*.
collected and edited by Marie Winn. Reprinted
by permission of Simon & Schuster. Inc.

For Walter and Bonnie,
with love

There's a hole in the bucket, dear Liza, dear Liza,
There's a hole in the bucket, dear Liza, a hole.

Well, fix it, dear Henry, dear Henry, dear Henry,
Well, fix it, dear Henry, dear Henry, fix it.

With what shall I fix it, dear Liza, dear Liza,
With what shall I fix it, dear Liza, with what?

With a straw, dear Henry, dear Henry, dear Henry,
With a straw, dear Henry, dear Henry, with a straw.

But the straw is too long, dear Liza, dear Liza,
But the straw is too long, dear Liza, too long.

Then cut it, dear Henry, dear Henry, dear Henry,
Then cut it, dear Henry, dear Henry, then cut it.

Well, how shall I cut it, dear Liza, dear Liza,
Well, how shall I cut it, dear Liza, well how?

With an axe, dear Henry, dear Henry, dear Henry,
With an axe, dear Henry, dear Henry, with an axe.

But the axe is too dull, dear Liza, dear Liza,
But the axe is too dull, dear Liza, too dull.

Then sharpen it, dear Henry, dear Henry, dear Henry,
Then sharpen it, dear Henry, dear Henry, then sharpen it.

On what shall I sharpen it, dear Liza, dear Liza,
On what shall I sharpen it, dear Liza, on what?

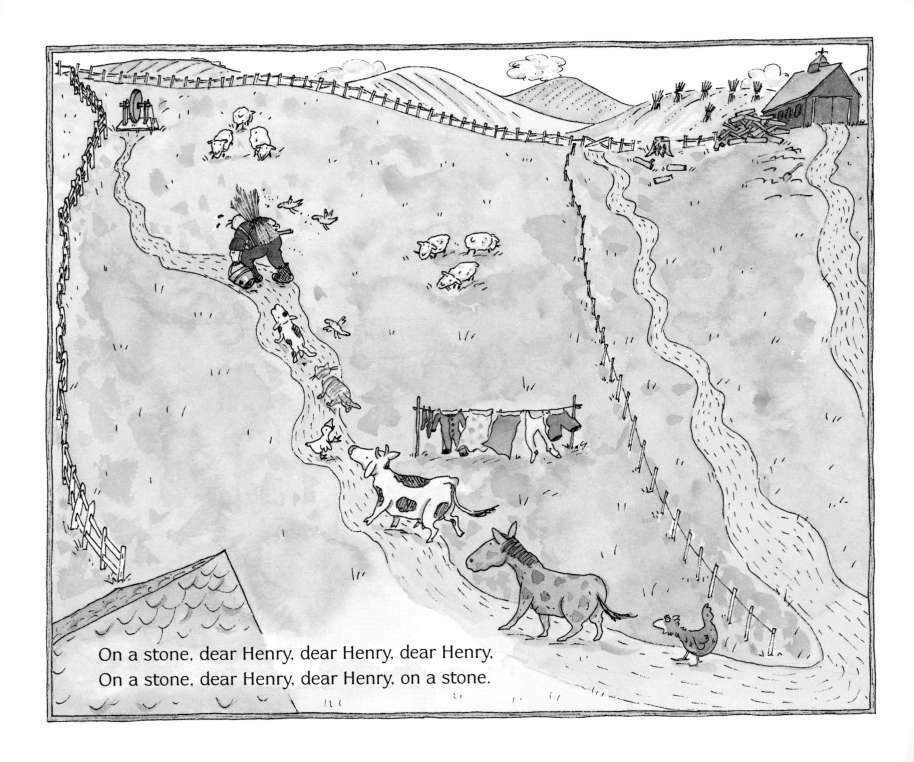

On a stone, dear Henry, dear Henry, dear Henry,
On a stone, dear Henry, dear Henry, on a stone.

But the stone is too dry, dear Liza, dear Liza,
But the stone is too dry, dear Liza, too dry.

Then wet it, dear Henry, dear Henry, dear Henry,
Then wet it, dear Henry, dear Henry, then wet it.

With what shall I wet it, dear Liza, dear Liza,
With what shall I wet it, dear Liza, with what?

With water, dear Henry, dear Henry, dear Henry,
With water, dear Henry, dear Henry, with water.

Well, how shall I carry it, dear Liza, dear Liza,
Well, how shall I carry it, dear Liza, well how?

In a bucket, dear Henry, dear Henry, dear Henry,
In a bucket, dear Henry, dear Henry, in a bucket.

BUT THERE'S A HOLE IN THE BUCKET, DEAR LIZA, DEAR LIZA,
THERE'S A HOLE IN THE BUCKET, DEAR LIZA, A HOLE.

Traditional
arr. Ray Kimmelman

With spirit

There's a hole in the buck-et, dear Li - za, dear
Well __ fix it, dear __ Hen-ry, dear Hen-ry, dear

Li - za, there's a hole in the buck-et, dear Li - za, a hole.
Hen - ry, well __ fix it, dear __ Hen-ry, dear Hen-ry, fix it.